Congregational
Systems Inventory

Understanding Your Congregation As A System

GEORGE PARSONS & SPEED B. LEAS

An Alban Institute Publication

First Rowman & Littlefield paperback edition 2014

Published by Rowman & Littlefield
4501 Forbes Blvd, Suite 200, Lanham, MD 20706
www.rowman.com

10 Thornbury Road, Plymouth PL6 7PP, United Kingdom

Library of Congress Cataloging-in-Publication Data Available

ISBN 13: 978-1-56699-121-6 (pbk: alk. paper)

☉™ The paper used in this publication meets the minimum requirements of American National Standard for Information Sciences—Permanence of Paper for Printed Library Materials, ANSI/NISO Z39.48-1992.

Printed in the United States of America

Table of Contents

5   Inventory Instructions

7   Congregational Systems Inventory

15   Scoring Instructions

17   Scoring Sheet – Part I

19   Scoring Sheet – Part II

21   Introduction to Congregational Systems Theory

21   Interpreting Your Scores

23   Strategy

24   Authority

25   Process

26   Pastoral Leadership

27   Relatedness

28   Lay Leadership

29   Learning

Inventory Instructions

- In each pair of choices, check the response that *most clearly* describes your congregation, even if neither choice is completely accurate.

- Focus on your congregation as it is *currently*, not how it used to be or how you wish it to be.

- There are no right or wrong choices. Give your first impression.

- Make a choice for every pair. If you check neither option or both options, the inventory results will be invalid.

- Terminology:

    "Lay leader" refers to those serving on the Board and those heading committees or other groups in the congregation.

    "Pastor" refers to the paid, ordained clergyperson or head of staff (on multiple staff). NOTE: If your congregation has a co-pastor (equals) arrangement, you may want to complete those items twice.

Congregational Systems Inventory

1. a._____ As a congregation, we have a clear, overall plan that we follow together.
    b._____ As a congregation, we encourage boards or committees to create and follow their own plans.

2. a._____ Decisions in our congregation tend to be influenced by many groups and many individuals.
    b._____ Decisions in our congregation tend to be influenced by a few groups or individuals.

3. a._____ Committee members do what they are expected to do.
    b._____ Committee members take initiative to define their responsibilities.

4. a._____ Our pastor places emphasis on producing new directions for ministry.
    b._____ Our pastor places emphasis on organizing the resources to develop current directions.

5. a._____ In the extreme, our congregation might overemphasize mutual agreement to the detriment of creative ideas.
    b._____ In the extreme, our congregation might overemphasize individual creativity to the detriment of good team decisions.

6. a._____ Sometimes our lay leaders overfocus on the larger vision and lose sight of the basic management of the congregation.
    b._____ Sometimes our lay leaders overfocus on cost, budget, and building maintenance and lose sight of the larger picture.

7. a._____ Our leadership (clergy and laity together) stays with tried and true approaches to ministry.
    b._____ Our leadership (clergy and laity together) introduces new programs and approaches to ministry on a regular basis.

8. a._____ Our planning process is informal and varies from year to year.
    b._____ Our planning process tends to be well organized and consistent.

9.   a._____   We have some entrenched groups or individuals that tend to run things around here.

       b._____   We are so concerned about consensus and collaboration that we suffer for a lack of decisive leadership.

10.   a._____   Committee members feel pretty much on their own to get what they need to do their work.

       b._____   Committee members know what is expected of them and where they can go for assistance and resources.

11.   a._____   Our pastor organizes people to carry out plans.

       b._____   Our pastor motivates people by inspiring them to join together.

12.   a._____   When engaged in the work of ministry, we expect people to come forth with dissenting points of view.

       b._____   When engaged in the work of ministry, we expect people to work as part of harmonious team.

13.   a._____   Most of our lay leaders are likely to place greater emphasis on the practicalities of today.

       b._____   Most of our lay leaders are likely to place greater emphasis on the possibilities of tomorrow.

14.   a._____   Our leadership (clergy and laity together) places emphasis on learning to do new things well.

       b._____   Our leadership (clergy and laity together) places emphasis on improving what we already do well.

15.   a._____   Sometimes I think we spend too much time planning.

       b._____   Sometimes I think we spend too little time planning.

16.   a._____   We bring new people into leadership roles on a regular basis.

       b._____   Leadership in our congregation is recycled among the same circle.

17.   a._____   We have regular ways, understood by everyone, for passing information from one group to another.

       b._____   We rely on people's best judgment about what information needs to be passed from group to group.

18. a._____ Our pastor leads by inspiring people to create change.
    b._____ Our pastor leads by guiding people to do systematic problem solving.

19. a._____ In general our leaders would be characterized as team players.
    b._____ In general our leaders would be characterized as individualists (soloists who team up when necessary).

20. a._____ Most of our lay leaders place an emphasis on producing new directions for ministry.
    b._____ Most of our lay leaders place an emphasis on organizing our resources to develop current directions.

21. a._____ Our leadership (clergy and laity together) is putting more effort into developing our *current* strengths as a congregation.
    b._____ Our leadership (clergy and laity together) is putting more effort into developing *new* strengths as a congregation.

22. a._____ We tend to re-vision our direction from time to time.
    b._____ We tend to do pretty much the same things each year.

23. a._____ Among our lay leaders we have some real standouts who have greatly influenced our decisions.
    b._____ Among our lay leaders we have many capable people but no real standouts.

24. a._____ Each part of our congregation is relatively uninformed about what the others are doing.
    b._____ Each part of our congregation usually knows what the other parts are doing.

25. a._____ Our pastor focuses first on making the organization work.
    b._____ Our pastor focuses first on transforming the organization.

26. a._____ We expect groups to contend and produce "minority reports" if necessary.
    b._____ We expect groups in our church to seek consensus whenever possible.

27. a._____ Most of our lay leaders are likely to make decisions on the basis of organizational practicalities.
    b._____ Most of our lay leaders are likely to make decisions on the basis of ideals.

28. a._____ A motto that would describe our approach to ministry is "nothing ventured, nothing gained."

    b._____ A motto that would describe our approach to ministry is "stay the course."

29. a._____ Our lay leaders are committed to a long-range plan.

    b._____ Our lay leaders are willing to change the plans in response to changing circumstances.

30. a._____ We tend to emphasize participation in our music program.

    b._____ We tend to emphasize excellence in our music program.

31. a._____ Committees, boards, and other program groups know their responsibilities and their range of authority.

    b._____ Committees, boards, and other program groups tend to be unclear about their responsibilities and range of authority.

32. a._____ As a leader, our pastor emphasizes new directions and change.

    b._____ As a leader, our pastor emphasizes good administration and organization.

33. a._____ In our congregation people value group effort and are cautious about excessive individualism.

    b._____ In our congregation people value individual initiative and are cautious about excessive collaboration.

34. a._____ Most of our lay leaders inspire people to create change.

    b._____ Most of our lay leaders guide people to do systematic problem solving.

35. a._____ Programatically, our leadership (clergy and laity together) tends to repeat the same things year to year.

    b._____ Programatically, our leadership (clergy and laity together) tends to go with the trends.

36. a._____ Our overall direction as a congregation is unclear.

    b._____ Our overall direction as a congregation is clear.

37. a._____ We are more comfortable letting decisive leaders shape our ministry.

    b._____ We are more comfortable including as many people as possible in the shaping of our ministry.

38. a._____ Decision-making ability varies a good deal from committee to committee.
     b._____ Boards and committees use consistent and reliable ways of making decisions.

39. a._____ Our pastor is a detail person who values results.
     b._____ Our pastor is a visioning person who values change.

40. a._____ When it comes to the work of ministry, our usual strategy is to divide up the tasks and set people free to get the job done.
     b._____ When it comes to the work of ministry, our usual strategy is to do most everything in committee.

41. a._____ Most of our lay leaders focus first on making the organization work.
     b._____ Most of our lay leaders focus first on transforming the organization.

42. a._____ When it comes to trying new approaches to ministry, our leaders (clergy and laity together) are likely to be risk takers.
     b._____ When it comes to trying new approaches to ministry, our leaders (clergy and laity together) are likely not to take risks.

43. a._____ We believe it's better to follow a carefully developed plan.
     b._____ We believe it's better to remain open to changing needs and opportunities.

44. a._____ Our members question leaders (pastor(s) and Board) frequently.
     b._____ Our members do not question leaders (pastor(s) and Board).

45. a._____ When it comes to getting things done, our congregation tends to emphasize policies and procedures.
     b._____ When it comes to getting things done, our congregation tends to emphasize individual freedom and initiative.

46. a._____ Our pastor tends to focus on longer-term goals.
     b._____ Our pastor tends to focus on shorter-term goals.

47. a._____ We sometimes sacrifice individual initiative to preserve our fellowship.
     b._____ We sometimes sacrifice harmony to encourage the autonomy of groups and individuals.

48.   a._____   Most of our lay leaders emphasize new directions and change.
      b._____   Most of our lay leaders emphasize good administration and organization.

49.   a._____   At our worst our congregation might be described as stuck in the same old ruts.
      b._____   At our worst our congregation might be described as a jack of all trades, master of none.

50.   a._____   Our congregation's direction and priorities are shaped by current needs and issues.
      b._____   Our congregation's directions and priorities are determined by a long-range plan.

51.   a._____   Most important decisions in our congregation are made by those at the top.
      b._____   Most important decisions in our congregation are made at the grass-roots.

52.   a._____   Within our congregation's leadership (clergy and laity together) new ideas or proposals tend to get a welcome hearing and can be quickly adopted if they have merit.
      b._____   Within our congregation's leadership (clergy and laity together) new ideas or proposals are taken through a series of steps and given lengthy consideration before adoption.

53.   a._____   Our pastor is devoted to helping people develop a careful plan and then methodically bringing the plan into action.
      b._____   Our pastor is devoted to helping people catch a vision and then move together toward that vision.

54.   a._____   Groups within our congregation tend to compete.
      b._____   Groups within our congregation tend to cooperate.

55.   a._____   Most of our lay leaders are detail-oriented people who value results.
      b._____   Most of our lay leaders are visionary people who value change.

56.   a._____   Our congregation is likely to launch new experiments in ministry.
      b._____   Our congregation is likely to gradually build on past successes in ministry.

57. a._____ We set goals and expect them to be attained.
    b._____ We set goals but often forget about them.

58. a._____ We have evolved a participatory and collaborative decision-making process in our congregation.
    b._____ We have evolved an efficient chain of command in our congregation.

59. a._____ Within our congregation's leadership (clergy and laity together) we have a clear system for receiving, addressing, and solving problems that arise.
    b._____ Within our congregation's leadership (clergy and laity together) we handle problems that arise on a case by case basis.

60. a._____ Our pastor is at her/his best when challenging us toward some new direction.
    b._____ Our pastor is at her/his best when keeping the structures of our congregation working smoothly.

61. a._____ Once decisions are made we expect people to support those decisions.
    b._____ Once decisions are made we allow room for dissent.

62. a._____ Most of our lay leaders tend to focus on longer-term goals.
    b._____ Most of our lay leaders tend to focus on shorter-term goals.

63. a._____ We have stayed too long with a few successful projects or programs.
    b._____ We fragment ourselves with too many new projects and programs.

64. a._____ We undercommit to our plans by not identifying and pursuing clear, measurable outcomes.
    b._____ We overcommit to our plans by not considering new opportunities along the way.

65. a._____ Some committees or working groups in our congregation tend to dominate the others.
    b._____ Working groups and units in our congregation tend to cooperate with one another.

66. a._____ Our members are not likely to know where and how to lodge a complaint, concern, or criticism.
    b._____ Our members are likely to know where and how to lodge a complaint, concern, or criticism.

67. a._____   Our pastor is likely to place greater emphasis on the practicalities of today.

     b._____   Our pastor is likely to place greater emphasis on the possibilities of tomorrow.

68. a._____   We do little to monitor the performance of our committees and program groups.

     b._____   We endeavor to monitor the performance of our committees and program groups.

69. a._____   Most of our lay leadership tends to be realistic.

     b._____   Most of our lay leadership tends to be idealistic.

70. a._____   Changing circumstances over the years have led us to develop new capabilities for ministry.

     b._____   Changing circumstances over the years have led us to enhance proven capabilities for ministry.

STEP #1

Transfer the check marks from your inventory to the corresponding boxes on the Scoring Sheet – Part I. Leave the box *blank* when the response indicated was *not* checked.

Example:

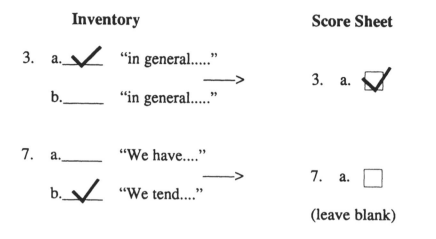

| Inventory | Score Sheet |

STEP #2

Add the total number of boxes containing check marks in each column.

STEP #3

Transfer column totals to Scoring Sheet – Part II.

Scoring Sheet — Part I

1.b ☐   2.a ☐   3.b ☐   4.a ☐   5.b ☐   6.a ☐   7.b ☐

8.a ☐   9.b ☐   10.a ☐   11.b ☐   12.a ☐   13.b ☐   14.a ☐

15.b ☐   16.a ☐   17.b ☐   18.a ☐   19.b ☐   20.a ☐   21.b ☐

22.a ☐   23.b ☐   24.a ☐   25.b ☐   26.a ☐   27.b ☐   28.a ☐

29.b ☐   30.a ☐   31.b ☐   32.a ☐   33.b ☐   34.a ☐   35.b ☐

36.a ☐   37.b ☐   38.a ☐   39.b ☐   40.a ☐   41.b ☐   42.a ☐

43.b ☐   44.a ☐   45.b ☐   46.a ☐   47.b ☐   48.a ☐   49.b ☐

50.a ☐   51.b ☐   52.a ☐   53.b ☐   54.a ☐   55.b ☐   56.a ☐

57.b ☐   58.a ☐   59.b ☐   60.a ☐   61.b ☐   62.a ☐   63.b ☐

64.a ☐   65.b ☐   66.a ☐   67.b ☐   68.a ☐   69.b ☐   70.a ☐

Total

Strategy	Authority	Process	Pastoral Leadership	Relatedness	Lay Leadership	Learning

Scoring Sheet — Part II

STRATEGY

Planned   • • • • • • • • • • •   Spontaneous
0 1 2 3 4 5 6 7 8 9 10

AUTHORITY

Concentrated   • • • • • • • • • • •   Dispersed
0 1 2 3 4 5 6 7 8 9 10

PROCESS

Mandatory   • • • • • • • • • • •   Discretionary
0 1 2 3 4 5 6 7 8 9 10

PASTORAL LEADERSHIP

Managerial   • • • • • • • • • • •   Transformational
0 1 2 3 4 5 6 7 8 9 10

RELATEDNESS

Collegial   • • • • • • • • • • •   Individual
0 1 2 3 4 5 6 7 8 9 10

LAY LEADERSHIP

Managerial   • • • • • • • • • • •   Transformational
0 1 2 3 4 5 6 7 8 9 10

LEARNING

Maximize   • • • • • • • • • • •   Metamize
0 1 2 3 4 5 6 7 8 9 10

Introduction to Congregational Systems Theory

All organizations live between the excesses of chaos and overcontrol. Congregations are likely to be at their best when they maintain a healthy tension between the requirements of living in community (integration) and the need in each person to be an individual (differentiation).

Living in tension means living with contention. When the level of contention drops too low, congregations tend to become frozen or brittle. No challenge means patterns of doing and thinking become too rigid. On the other hand, too much change or contention can also be a problem. When anger levels are high or we don't know what to expect next, life in a congregation can be chaotic and the organization loses its ability to get on with its work.

We have selected seven dimensions of a congregation's system. In each dimension a healthy tension is needed in your congregation. At both ends of each dimension we have placed valued tendencies or polarities. These contending opposites are *both* needed for effective and vital congregational functioning. The challenge is to live in the tension between these opposites and to use the tension as a source of energy for ongoing renewal.

Interpreting Your Scores

Your response to the inventory produces a score between 0 and 10 for each dimension. Placed on the continuum for each dimension, your scores indicate the degree of relative tension that currently exists in your congregation.

Scores plotted toward the center (4-6) would indicate an approximation of optimum tension between contending opposites.

Scores plotted toward one end (0-3) or the other (7-10) would indicate a loss of tension and a dominance by one opposite or the risk of excessive reliance on that tendency.

Looking at these dimensions *in relation to one another* will provide important clues for your change efforts as leaders.

You will gain a more complete assessment of your congregation by "pooling" the scores of a group of lay leaders and staff and creating a combined score for each dimension.

Strategy

Definition: Strategy is the way congregations put their vision into practice. This dimension might also be called planning or mission.

PLANNED . . . . .SPONTANEOUS

Developing a clear sense of purpose and direction...
Connecting goals and objectives to that purpose...
Bringing organizational criteria to bear on the evaluation of ministry...

Maintaining an openness to God's leading...
Remaining responsive to emerging opportunities and needs...
Using members' gifts and talents flexibly...

Excesses at the Planned End of the Scale

— Congregation's field of vision is limited to "what fits the plan."
— Ongoing planning process absorbs leader's time and energy.
— Management by objectives process is more important than the objectives.
— Inability to respond to new opportunities or new needs.
— Looking good on paper replaces effectiveness.
— Spontaneous leaders lose interest or are driven out.

Excesses at the Spontaneous End of the Scale

— Goals may be defined at a planning retreat but then forgotten.
— Congregational identity or direction is unclear.
— Leadership is vulnerable to current trends and fads.
— Congregational projects become disconnected from one another.
— Lack of goal agreement produces repetitive conflicts.
— Matching needs of the congregation with clergy skills is guess work.

Living in the Tension

— The congregation knows its goals and priorities.
— Members are conscious of this year's priorities.
— The leadership is in agreement about the goals.
— Clergy leadership is selected on the basis of the congregation's clear sense of identity and direction.
— Resources are used in relation to the goals and priorities.
— Creative initiatives that may not fit the plans are sought and encouraged.
— Envisioning activity is done on a regular basis.
— Leadership is regularly studying the congregation's environment.
— The congregation's grass roots are consulted.
— A spirit of open inquiry is created to periodically reshape the plans.
— Leadership treats unplanned exigencies as opportunities.

Authority

Definition: Authority is the ability to influence decision-making in the congregation. This dimension refers to the extent to which authority is concentrated in the hands of a few people or dispersed to larger groups or the entire congregation.

CONCENTRATED. . . . . DISPERSED

Shaping ministry with decisive leadership...
Empowering talented groups and individuals to act...
Maintaining consistency in leadership roles...

Consulting the larger congregation about important issues...
Bringing new people into leadership roles...
Encouraging "grass roots" decision making...

Excesses at the Concentrated End of the Scale

— Small groups or individuals have the "power" to derail leadership decisions.
— Leadership is recycled; new people are excluded.
— Power groups become entrenched and dominate others.
— In-group/out-group phenomenon develops.
— Those with authority become blind to their impact on others.

Excesses at the Dispersed End of the Scale

— People are confused about who makes which decisions.
— Leaders are rotated, discouraging competency development.
— Strong leadership is distrusted.
— The decision-making process is slow.
— Individuals are reluctant to come forward to lead.
— Consensus decisions create lowest common denominator results.

Living in the Tension

— Talented people can function interdependently.
— Groups and individuals are given permission to use their power.
— Lay leaders stay in a position long enough to develop expertise but have time limits and "sabbaticals."
— The official leaders (staff and Board) are able to give clear leadership while staying in touch with the congregation.
— New people are brought into positions of authority.
— People with expertise are given authority and responsibility.
— Competing groups or individuals are brought together to work cross-functionally.
— The range of authority granted to individuals or groups is clearly defined and periodically re-evaluated.
— The exercise of authority in congregational life is a subject for periodic discussion.

Process

Definition: Process refers to the information sharing and decision-making procedures in a congregation and the extent to which these procedures are clearly defined and regulated or variable and left to the discretion of individuals.

MANDATORY. . . . . DISCRETIONARY

Developing and following clear
guidelines for decision making...
Providing a conflict management map...
Connecting the parts of the congregation
with good information flow...

Encouraging individual initiative
toward problem solving...
Allowing grace (love) to supersede
law (rules)...
Adapting decision-making processes
to fit the siuation...

Excesses at the Mandatory End of the Scale

— Operating procedures become rigid and awkward.
— Leadership becomes obsessed with following the rules.
— Creativity is stifled, especially regarding how the congregation can better do the work of ministry.
— Staff become burdened with monitoring policies and procedures.

Excesses at the Discretionary End of the Scale

— People don't know their part in the work of the organization.
— Members don't know what the Board or its various committees are doing.
— People don't know where to take a problem or lodge a complaint.
— Committees lack clear assignments and a defined range of authority.
— People don't know what to do when a person or group behaves inappropriately.
— Committees lack clear agendas and do not hold people accountable for assigned responsibilities.

Living in the Tension

— Members are expected to follow the rules but apply rules with some flexibility.
— Policies and procedures are re-examined periodically so that they accurately reflect the congregation's values.
— Lay leaders and staff have clear guidelines for handling problems and complaints, but also exercise discretion.
— The congregation has adopted a clearly defined conflict management strategy.
— Committees and work groups have job descriptions and know their range of authority.
— Leaders are trained to conduct effective, efficient, and user-friendly meetings.
— Leaders know who is to be consulted or informed regarding particular decisions.

Pastoral Leadership

Definition: Pastoral leadership is the ability of the pastor(s) to generate *intended* change in an organization.

MANAGERIAL .... TRANSFORMATIONAL

Organizing resources to develop current directions...
Guiding people to do systematic problem solving...
Focusing on practical results in the short run...

Shaping a vision for new directions...
Inspiring people to create change...

Focusing on future possibilities...

Excesses at the Managerial End of the Scale

— Pastors develop tunnel vision focused on the control of resources and programs.
— Risk taking in the congregation is reduced.
— Keeping things running smoothly overshadows larger purposes.
— Short-term practicalities dominate decision making.
— Creative possibilities have to be "run through the planning process."
— Transformational staff and lay leaders are viewed as "loose cannons."

Excesses at the Transformational End of the Scale

— Pastors don't tie vision to practical issues.
— Changes are constantly introduced at the expense of time-tested strengths and approaches.
— Core purposes of the congregation are obscured by fragmented change efforts.
— Pastors are too far "out in front" and lose touch with the membership.
— Managerial staff and lay leaders are characterized as rigid.
— Oversight of the congregation's structural and institutional needs is neglected.

Living in the Tension

— The vision is well managed.
— The pastor encourages an ongoing discussion about how much change and risk to introduce and when to stay the course.
— The pastor leads efforts to keep differing leadership styles in dialogue.
— The pastor is willing to take risks toward new directions and stay in touch with the congregation while doing so.
— Pastors who reside strongly at one end of the continuum seek the counsel and advice of those who reside at the opposite end.
— Changes introduced in the life of the congregation are accompanied by the necessary staffing, budgeting, leadership oversight.
— Pastors on one side of the leadership dimension seek continuing education opportunities to develop the other side.

Relatedness

Definition: Relatedness is the way members of an organization work together, especially whether their work is done cooperatively or independently.

COLLEGIAL . . . . INDIVIDUAL

Encouraging cooperative efforts to do the work of ministry...	Placing a premium on individual initiative...
Collaborating to make decisions as a team...	Freeing individuals and smaller groups to pursue their calling...
Emphasizing team play and harmonious relationship...	Encouraging the free expression of ideas...

Excesses at the Collegial End of the Scale

— Everything is done in committees.
— An overconcern for preserving relationships results in an "enmeshed system"; conflict is suppressed.
— People are unable to state clearly what they need from others to do their work.
— Changes come slowly since many need to be consulted and most need to agree.
— Those willing to risk dissent are labeled as troublemakers.

Excesses at the Individual End of the Scale

— Patience and stamina to work collaborative decisions is limited.
— The division of labor among leaders creates "turf" issues and a loss of coordination.
— Antagonistic tribes engage in power struggles with one another.
— Relationship "glue" is weakened; a disengaged system develops.
— Open conflict becomes a pastime.

Living in the Tension

— People are expected to take the initiative, but explore its impact on others.
— The work of individuals and smaller groups is tied to the overall purposes of the congregation and the work is reviewed.
— Collaborative decision making is encouraged where possible, but dissent and "minority reports" are expected.
— Leaders are encouraged to face differences around the issues of congregational life while taking care of one another in the midst of those differences.
— Committees and work groups are large enough to get good samples of opinion, but small enough to get the work done.
— Committees are given an adequate range of authority so that the Board does not often act as a committee of the whole.
— People are valued. Work groups devote time to relationship building and spiritual development.

Lay Leadership

Definition: Lay leadership is the ability of lay leaders to generate *intended* change in an organization.

MANAGERIAL . . . . TRANSFORMATIONAL

Organizing people to do their part toward the larger goals...	Helping members capture a vision or new directions...
Overseeing projects and committees to insure task completion...	Inspiring people to create change...
Focusing on practical results in the short run...	Focusing on future possibilities...

Excesses at the Managerial End of the Scale

— The Board develops tunnel vision, focusing only on "maintenance" needs.
— Leaders discourage creative or innovative ideas.
— Transformational staff and lay leaders are ignored or excluded.
— Leaders react to current demands and are not able to look into the future.
— Danger signals (declining financial support or Sunday attendance, changing neighborhood, emerging conflict among membership) are ignored in favor of meeting current goals.

Excesses at the Transformational End of the Scale

— Lay leaders sacrifice good stewardship of the congregation's resources in favor of new programs or projects.
— Risk-taking endeavors are not grounded in good management.
— Change efforts in the congregation are disconnected and poorly organized.
— The Board repeatedly misjudges the congregation's willingness and ability to adapt to change initiatives.
— Managerial staff and lay leaders are characterized as rigid bureaucrats and are excluded from leadership circles.

Living in the Tension

— The Board and other lay leaders put forth a clear vision for the congregation's future and they manage that vision into reality.
— Those who recruit lay leaders look for both kinds of leadership.
— Managerial and transformational lay leaders are both represented on Boards and committees and efforts are made to encourage the acceptance of one by the other.
— Lay leaders are helped to become visionaries and not fill assigned slots.
— Change initiatives are accompanied by good management.
— Leaders are willing to take risks toward new directions and stay in touch with the membership while doing so.

The Alban Institute

Learning

Definition: Learning is a congregation's orientation toward the past or future as it experiments with improving its life and ministry.

MAXIMIZE. . . . . METAMIZE

Building on the congregation's strengths...
Learning from past successes to develop the future...
Enhancing the congregation's distinctive competencies...

Going beyond current strengths to develop something new...
Learning from that which is new and untried...
Building new competencies that are discontinuous with the past...

Excesses at the Maximizing End of the Scale

— Past successes have become present ruts.
— People with new ideas or approaches become discouraged.
— Incremental improvements in existing programs and processes lull congregational leaders into believing that they are effectively responding to the needs of the membership and the community.
— Environmental changes catch the congregation by surprise.

Excesses at the Metamizing End of the Scale

— The congregation is vulnerable to current trends and fads.
— Leaders neglect or abandon basic strengths of their congregation.
— Leaders initiate discontinuous change without bringing the congregation along; the leadership becomes isolated.
— Creative experiments in ministry fragment the congregation, increase discord, and cause the tradition bound members to entrench.
— The congregation runs the risk of losing its identity as a result of the changes.
— Experimental programs are initiated without adequate resources.

Living in the Tension

— Leaders know what the congregation's current "distinctive competencies" are and help the congregation celebrate these gifts from God.
— The congregation is slow to abandon successful ministries but regularly experiments with new opportunities for ministry.
— Maximizing and metamizing voices are kept in dialogue.
— Leaders recognize that developing a new congregational strength takes time; adequate time lines and evaluation procedures are established to avoid premature abandonment of an experiment.
— New projects are connected to a long-range plan.